Ancient Memories
New Beginnings

By the same author
The World Beyond Today
Adventure into Transformation

Ancient Memories
New Beginnings

Merriene Scott

with her spiritual messengers
from Illanitis

Published by Merriene Scott
Email: merriene@merrienescott.com

First published 2004
Ancient Memories, New Beginnings is the third book of a trilogy,
'Messages from Illanitis'.

National Library of Australia
Cataloguing-in-Publication entry

Scott, Merriene.
The world beyond today:
a guide to your multidimensional future.

ISBN 978-0-9751058-7-0
eBook: 978-0-646-72981-7
1. Spiritualism. 2. Self-actualisation (Psychology).
I. Title. (Series: Scott, Merriene.
Messages from Illanitis; bk. 3).
133.93

Typeset in 13/19 Bembo
Printed by Optima Digital Print, Perth
Cover image by Jamie Scott (www.jamiescottimages.com)

This book is dedicated to those of you who are
seeking to be all that you truly are living fully
to reach your unique, exquisite potential.

And to my mother, Elsie McKenzie,
with love and deep respect.

Contents

Acknowledgments

My loving gratitude to Irene Percy, who has enthusiastically and very patiently transferred my handwriting into clear type.

I am also indebted to Allan Watson for his wonderful eye for detail as he diligently edited the book. His perceptive advice has been greatly appreciated.

To my family and friends, thank you for your support and love.

With gentle and loving cooperation from my unseen divine friends, these three teaching journals – the now completed trilogy – have been created.

I am grateful for the honour of being part of this manifestation.

About the Front Cover

The flower mandala was created by my son Jamie Scott from a photograph he took of a single Australian wildflower, *Scaevola* (fan flower). The completed design has within it many images of the magic of creation.

The invitation is there for you to see the devas, elves, fairies and other wonderful beings who have their essence within the mandala's shapes and colours. The portal in its centre invites you into your new beginning.

'A portal is a spiritual energy door – an opening that allows the Human to connect to wisdom. Each Human Being, on their own, with intent, may access the portal, and walk through the new door. And through the portal is an advancement, a catalyst, a *three* of wisdom: solution, inner peace and, yes, even of joy.'

The Kryon Writings – The New Beginning
Copyright © 2002

Preface

Ancient Memories, New Beginnings completes a trilogy that began with an exploration of the truth of being in *The World Beyond Today* and continued with *Adventure into Transformation*, a further investigation and reflection on love, wisdom and changing perceptions.

We complete the exploration in this book, with each of us being encouraged to go deeper into our own truth of existence and find the magic.

As well as being a great privilege, my own journey in writing this trilogy – by automatic writing with my spiritual friends from higher levels of knowing – has brought me much insight and inspiration. It has spanned six years, during which I have had many months away from writing as my life has been experienced in other ways: the death of a close friend, the birth of three precious grandchildren and travel to other parts of the world, where I have shared wonderful experiences with some beautiful souls. Trusting the slow process has opened the way to greater awareness and understanding in the meantime.

I have been lovingly assisted in writing this book by Isis, who waited patiently for me to be ready. A dear friend of mine, with a deep knowledge of myth and a wise interpreter of dreams, received the message that the Universal Goddess Isis was there to work with me on this project. It took some encouragement, however, for me to make contact with her.

From prehistoric times Isis has been identified as the universal mother, sovereign of all things and the single manifestation of all. With trust and willingness I merged wondrously with her to become the messenger of the love, truth and beauty revealed in the following pages. The gene of Isis, the Genesis, being awakened within my pineal gland (third eye), enabled me to access my soul memory (what <u>is</u> is).

Over time I have come to understand the 'place' from where the messages have come for this trilogy. *Illanitis*, mentioned at the beginning of each book, is a *feeling within* – of being in the present moment – and yet awakening the memories of all our lives experienced in eternity (I <u>llan</u> it <u>is</u>).

We each have Isis and Illanitis within just waiting to be activated and honoured, allowing us to open up to the true freedom of just *being*.

My blessings are with you on your own journey of discovery and recognition of your unique contribution to the continuing evolution of humanity – and of existence as a whole.

Merriene Scott

Introduction

May your life be rich and meaningful. You have the joy within you for this to be so. You have the memories within of who you truly are, and joy will come as you unlock those memories and thus have full access to this person who is you.

We are the messengers from Illanitis and are here to bring about this change in you. As we assist you to unlock the ancient memories held deep within, we manifest a magical transformation of all that has held you back in your knowing.

Your knowing is there within. Much has been hidden from your heart through the control held over you by your conditioning and your limited understanding of yourself as a human being.

Many people are now much more conscious of their uniqueness as a human, and understand they have no need to be the same as others. You are a soul of both great worth and great wisdom, and it only needs you to acknowledge this to release the mystery of the knowledge held within.

This book is a journey into your ancient memories of your origins as a species and a wake-up message to manifest the power you possess within. Please accept our ideas and thoughts as triggers to explore your own truth. Understand that your memories and concepts of the meaning of life may be different to ours. With this reading you may unlock your own memories and find access to all that is true for you.

Our messages are messages of hope and great love. Do you remember the love you gave to us as you journeyed here to this physical existence? If you do not remember, we can remind you of this and reassure you how willing you were to come to be part of this phase of growth in human evolution. Your contract, signed with love and surrender to the experiences you have had and are having, was undertaken with great willingness – and might we say eagerness – for the opportunity to gain valuable knowledge in this plane of existence.

Most of you have forgotten this pledge and forgotten the love. With love all is achievable. Now we can return you to the feeling of love stored deep within your cells.

As you undertake this journey of reawakening your memories of love, you will once again transform into a being of greater light and transparency and therefore assist many others to look deep within themselves. As you notice the shift in perceptions within, a shift will also occur without.

You might have a new beginning in many areas of your life. You might change your work occupation, move house or even country and find a new companion with whom to share your journey. In some cases the shift will take you into a much deeper and more fulfilling relationship with the partner you currently have and enable you to have the most beautiful relationship with everything in existence – the earth, plants, animals and other people.

Much joy awaits you in this journey into yourself, taken through our mystical messages and triggers of memory. We join you with much love and honour as you read.

Chapter One

Your transformation is now beginning. You may wonder how you are to know the outcome of this change. With the coming of many powerful new frequencies, you will begin to notice your transformation in the ways of physical difference as well as outlook on life.

Pause a moment and look in the mirror at the face you have always known. Through your growing years you studied this face to see the signs of maturity coming, and also followed the changing shape of your figure. Now, perhaps, you are so used to your face and body you no longer give it due respect and attention.

As you stare at your face in the mirror, allow your eyes to lose focus and you will see your soul looking at you through your face. We suggest that by lighting a candle and placing it close by, you illuminate the image of your soul, which is waiting to have more say in your present life. You may see many images of who you have been and will be as they flash in and out while you focus on your facial image. You may see yourself as very old or very young, or somewhere in between, and these are all you at other times, in other dimensions of yourself.

All of these memories are retained in your genetic coding and are now about to assist you in your transformation into a lighter and more knowing being. All you are is there in your face or the faces you are acknowledging in the mirror.

The face you have presented to your family and friends is the face of this lifetime only. You have buried deep within you, as they have within them, all the memories of every existence you have ever experienced. We suggest it is now time to bring to the surface your knowing of the memories and the wisdom retained for eternity within.

Our assistance now is to bring about your remembrance of who you truly are through the ideas we will present to you within these pages. The words used will be codes to reawaken the knowledge you have stored so well inside; on reading these code words the knowledge will be triggered open for you. Please understand magic will occur as you unravel your secrets within, bringing about your transformation into the new you of light and joy.

In the beginning of time, the planet Earth was evolving to a state of readiness for the arrival of humankind. When the conditions were perfect, the first seeds of humanity were planted on the Earth in the way of beings from far away in the Cosmos. The first humans were a cross, might we say, of other beings and a mutation of energy to create a new breed of being suitable to inhabit planet Earth. Perhaps you were there at the beginning and you have lived many times since – in various bodies in many different locations – to contribute to the evolution of humanity.

The early humans naturally were seemingly very primitive, as the Earth was a harsh environment. It has been necessary for humans to evolve at the same pace as the Earth, and now humanity has evolved to the level of possibly destroying itself, along with the planet that is your home.

You have all been part of this process and, in the cycles of life and death, you have experienced most of the emotions mankind has needed to gain the understanding necessary to move to the next level of existence, where you will have less dependence on your physical body. Your matter will be less dense and more fluid, creating a whole new species of human being.

Our role is to bring to you the tools and the knowledge of yourselves to create this change in you. We say this with great respect and knowing that you have only a few short steps to take to arrive at this new level of being.

Your deepest knowing is urging you on in your quest for completeness. You create the situations from which you will open up your awareness to much of what you have denied or ignored for so long.

For the most part mankind is still very young in terms of knowing of the greater picture of existence. Blocks and controls are created continuously to sabotage the growth of each soul. There are those of you and those of other energies who have a different agenda and wish to control the masses of mankind for your own reasons, these being reasons of manipulation – allowing you to stagnate and destroy yourselves as a species, preventing the ultimate glory of love from overriding fear-based existence.

We might say this is the dark of existence preventing the light from shining forth, as it ultimately will. May you understand love is all that is necessary to override fear and distrust in any situation. With love, all can be achieved and transformed. As you live with loving thoughts and actions, you raise your vibrations to a level that is not welcoming to fear and distrust. Therefore it has no power and no meaning any longer. Please remember this simple statement and you will achieve so much beyond your most beautiful dreams. You are far more than you think you are, and, in your time of discovery of your great gifts of intuition and deep knowing, the purpose of your present life will be revealed to you.

Those of you on the planet at this present time who are awake and consciously aware of who you truly are have special missions to accomplish for humanity. Do you know why *you* are here? Do you know *your* mission? Do you know the ultimate outcome of your mission?

Perhaps you have a sense of knowing; however you have pushed it deep down into your core and do not wish to be reminded of it. If this is the case, you will find situations continue to arise in which you are challenged once again to deal with them from your deepest core of knowing.

As you deal with your tests with great integrity, fairness and love, you will understand the key to all your wisdom is being revealed to the ultimate satisfaction and success of all concerned in the situation at hand. When you push away from finding the very best outcome for a situation, you are delaying your growth, and you will need to have another challenge similar to the previous one until you succeed in growing into wisdom.

How can you find out about yourself as an ancient being of great wisdom so that you can utilise the knowledge of your greater self in the transformation occurring for you?

We will assist with explaining the tools most useful for your discovery to occur. *Meditation* is an essential tool that will bring you to your soul, your core, your God/Goddess within, so you are tapping into your essence of self. The more often you meditate the stronger will be your relationship with your authentic beautiful self, who has all the answers to the questions of your ancient memories and will willingly share them with you – your personality (ego) self – as you give attention and willingness to it. In the silence your answers will be loud and clear.

The tool of meditating is the beginning of your *trust*. In trust you find your second tool. Within the knowing of who you truly are there is a little voice that will keep telling you the outcome of all you are dealing with. This voice we can call the voice of trust. Trust is the surrender to your inner knowing that all will be well for you as long as you act and think with integrity and love. Trust is the ability to let go of fear and allow the universe to assist in bringing about the outcome that is perfect for you. Trust is the letting go of any attachment to what the outcome might be, allowing you to relax into presentmoment dealings with the knowledge that you can trust whatever may happen to forces greater than yourself, your intentions always being for the highest good of all concerned.

The trust you give yourself to create all that you desire is a tool of enormous worth, and highly valuable in preparation for the ability to find your deepest memories of your truth.

All will begin to make sense to you when you can *let go of your fears* of everything in your life. This is another tool most useful in your preparation for a future you will enjoy having.

Fear is the stumbling-block to allowing abundance and understanding to manifest for you. Fear is created by your perceptions of what might be or what might happen. Of course as you fear you attract to you all that you fear, presenting the opportunities for these lower vibrations to affect you.

With trust you create very high vibrations, which leave no room for fearful thoughts or occurrences. Within every cell of your body you have these vibrations pulsating continuously and, with the feelings of love, joy and trust, they are of a resonance that tunes in with the universe of beauty and love.

This is the vibration connected with the essence of God and nature, which is the creation of harmony and balance in the Life Force. The vibration of fear is tuned to the darker side of the Life Force, and is necessary for protection and awareness of polarisation.

When the balance is tipped in favour of fearful existence, there is no longer a strong connection with the God essence of love and beauty.

Another tool necessary for you to use to awaken your deeply held memories is that of *understanding* – understanding of yourself as a spiritual being in a physical form here, in order to have the experiences necessary to bring your soul to a higher level of knowing. We have talked of this previously in our other books. We wish to reinforce how important this concept is in your perception of the nature of your existence.

As you swing your thinking around to this viewpoint, the importance of *doing* things diminishes and the importance of who and what you are *being* increases – the understanding of how significant your actions are and the intent behind those actions.

What is the purpose of your actions? Is it to help bring harmony and joy to others and yourself? Or is it to make money and further your advancement in the materialistic world? An action of kindness will reap far more rewards than an action of selfish advancement for yourself.

You have a desire to be needed and a desire to be loved. In these desires lie the yearnings for you to find your *worth*. Your worth is not about being the most popular or the wealthiest. It is about a feeling of *worthiness*. This worthiness is the reason for your existence. You all have a reason for being present now in this reality of your choosing, and your yearning is your attempt to remember your mission and why you have manifested at this time.

Each of you has a unique purpose and role to fulfil, and it may be very different from those of your other family members or current friends. This role you need to fulfil is your contribution to the journey home for humanity. Your contribution is very worthy, so we suggest your worthiness will be revealed as you follow your passion within and no longer look outside yourself to have your needs met.

No other person can fulfil your needs. That will happen as you listen to your heart, where your knowing is of the secret reason for your existence now in this third-dimensional reality. Your passion is your secret knowing; so, as you follow your deep passion, you will find that you accomplish your mission here.

Your *passion* is another tool for your rapid transformation. Following the very nature of the passionate feelings within will allow you to access your wisdom – your knowledge and remembrances of other times – where you may have been an expert in what is your greatest passion now.

The feelings of joy you may have as you paint a picture or sing in the shower are indications to you to pursue further these creative expressions within. Perhaps you love walking in the bush amongst the tall trees and by flowing rivers. You will be releasing many ancient memories of previous lives as you do so, and this will enable you to access other wisdoms simultaneously held within. Those who do not follow their passions are blocking the remembrance of their wisdom and preventing the commencement of the journey into their new beginning.

Without passion the will to grow is lost, and so those who deny this are stifled and confused as well as unhappy and negative in their outlook on life. We say please pay attention to finding your purpose; this will always incorporate everything you are passionate about. Think back to when you were a small child, and remember what you enjoyed doing and being most.

Many of you may have had your spontaneous passions subdued or stopped by unknowing parents. These are the core elements now needing to be expressed again to bring you into balance and harmony once more.

As you express your beautiful feelings in a way that is wonderfully fulfilling for you, there will occur openings in your energies to allow new, magical and mystical happenings to manifest in your world of being.

Without this opening of your heart, the new way of living cannot begin for you. It is in your *will* to allow this to happen, and it is as you wake up to who you truly are, in the process of following your passions, that you will transform.

Your will – your willpower – is a vital tool in allowing everything to change for those of you who are prepared to let go of the old worn-out ways of living and doing. Are you now ready to go on this journey further into the light, to be shown much you have not considered possible before?

Chapter Two

Existence is far, far greater than your three-dimensional existence, and in exploring further you will use your third-dimensional time much more wisely, graciously linking it in with your access to all other dimensions of your greater self.

Beyond your physicality lies an existence that involves much of your dreams and fantasies. With the coming of your deeper knowing and greater willingness, the portals to your other dimensions will open wide. You will access the senses you have had shut down for so long, and in this change will come your ability to be completely in your own power, with no one holding your strings, directing or manipulating you one way or another.

When you understand the God within you is all you need, you can let go of many religious beliefs and also old value structures imposed on you for so long by society's customs and rules. With the awakening of your own wonderful energies, long suppressed, the feelings gained will be those of strength, serenity, lightness and amazement in how you could have been asleep so long.

Does this surprise you? Do you understand what we are saying? Yes, most of you have been asleep most of your life, and living and acting in a robot fashion as you have dutifully followed those before you.

Many of you have not questioned the rules of government, the rules in your family paradigm or the rules you impose on yourself.

As you begin to question these rules, and start to bring about change in them through your own suggestions, the shift will occur on the planet for greater harmony and fairness. Everything in your life is reflected on the larger scale; in standing in your own power at all times you do make a difference.

With the coming changes, the old paradigms will no longer serve humanity. Eyes are being opened everywhere, and the unacceptable behaviour of many will no longer be acceptable to others or covered up by those wanting to find the easy way out. *You* have an influence in speaking your truth as you know it to be and, with the collective energies of wisdom speaking out, the rules will change for the benefit of all.

Your language will change and the words used will be words of insights and messages for those you are speaking to. With new language and new intentions in the words you use, understanding between the speaker and the listener will be far greater.

The power in the words will be taken into the heart of the listener and used to activate their feelings in regard to the message.

With the feelings will come a knowing of how to act or react appropriately with purity of thought and feeling combined. Until now most of humankind have acted or reacted to messages from others by replying from their thoughts only. Now the shift will be to always act with feeling thoughts that are more profound in every way.

The new era will also necessitate a change in ways of creating thoughts. In this process, a new dimension of knowledge will be brought in through your pineal gland, which is the centre of your spirituality and connection with the universal wisdom. Many of you know this as the third eye.

The third eye is your access to what lies in other dimensions and, with confidence, trust, willingness and openness, the activation will occur easily and naturally. With great respect to those of you who are already using your third eye regularly, we will now explain how this opening can be achieved for everyday use.

Firstly, we wish for you to meditate on this and state your intentions to activate into the other dimensions of yourself with love and trust, with the knowing of the responsibility this will bring. The responsibility is that of achieving your highest potential in this particular lifetime. It is not to be used or abused for reasons of greed or pride. It is to be used solely for attainment of your purpose, your passionate desire to manifest all that is for the highest good of mankind.

As you become fully attuned to the need to be humble and compassionate in all you do, we can then proceed to assist you to open up the portals to beyond the dimension of time and space reality, where you will choose your own destiny – that of creating the reality that is perfect for you.

The opening of your portal will occur as you use your tools of trust and your understanding of yourself as a greater being than the physical one you use as your vehicle. This is the vehicle you have created for use this lifetime of the now, and in this vehicle are the genetic codes of your memories to be accessed when you are ready.

You will be in a state of readiness when you create the desire and the passion to know more about the cellular memory stored deep within you. This curiosity will trigger the opening of your portal as you explore in your thinking the magnificence of the creation of the universe and all that is in it.

The birds are the messengers to this exploration. They are with you from the dimension of beauty and wisdom, and in their song is the music of the angels, allowing you to access the codes of remembrance. The birds are more than what they appear, as they have access within their being to the lineage and codes of creation. They have the inbuilt knowing of the way through the portals into immense information of a different kind than any you have ever experienced. They are the keepers of your souls and in their own way they bring magical energies to you, creating the opportunities for your changes into higher vibrations. Birdsong is of such a frequency that it can heal and change whatever is necessary when called on. Much of their work is unseen and unheralded in their daily appearances, and yet their ability to fly such long distances to arrive at a planned destination many thousands of miles from where they last were is unexplainable to most of you. They are in another dimension of energy, and they can easily sense their course and arrive exactly where they planned.

Do not forget that you too will have this ability as you move into higher frequencies on a regular basis. With dedicated thought and belief the transition will be very easy, with your new existence becoming a merger between your physical dimensions and all others. This merging will occur gradually when you let go of expectations that things occur in certain ways. All you need do is trust that you will be protected and taken only as far as your knowing will permit.

This merging begins as you meditate, with your discovery that you move into altered states of consciousness at these times. Many of you may teleport easily when you prepare yourself well, and give your intentions of the destination you wish to go to while your body remains behind.

Teleporting, for those of you who do not know, is the ability to take your subtle self anywhere you wish, and being there in subtle body (mind and spirit) absorbing the sounds, smells and views of the chosen destination. You will be as a ghost and not apparent to those in this other place. The time will be as normal, not in the past or the future.

All that is required to achieve teleporting is to relax, trust and give clear directions. Make sure you are in a safe, quiet place when you attempt this wonderful experience.

As your portal opens wide to new delights of your grander existence, we can bring in visions of the many other energies that are around you. These are the energies of other dimensions, which can only be seen as you rise in your frequencies and tune into them.

It is as with a radio or TV: you can only tune in to certain frequencies if your receiver is constructed to do so. Your body will now be constructed differently, and so be able to connect in at last to all that has always been there but you had not been adequately prepared to receive it. With your new attunement you will have much more finely adjusted senses and so will be able to see and hear much more.

With the coming of clearer vision (clairvoyance) the auras (energies) of those around you will be clearly visible and you will know much more about each person you are with. This will give you better insight into their state of feeling and thinking, and also their motives.

With the coming of the new energies the time is here to discard much of your previous ways, and by this we mean all of your old patterns of doing normal things, in parallel with a big change in your thinking about the way things are. You may begin to perceive very differently your habitual way of undertaking certain tasks, and suddenly see how you can do them more easily.

Perhaps you will have clearer insights into problems that have been troubling you for a long time, and will find that they can now be resolved effortlessly in no time at all. You may also come to a greater understanding of why a family member or friend behaves as they do: you will know the core of their issue very easily. As this understanding comes, you will find you are able to offer them assistance that helps bring their problem to an end very quickly.

Whatever the situation, change is inevitable, and no longer will the dynamics of energy exchange stay as they were. People will either disappear from your life or become more amenable and helpful in new ways.

No longer will the old 'rules' apply in government regulations, and in this we mean all levels from local councils through to national governments. No longer will those who wield the power be able to get away with short cuts and bestowing questionable favours. The time is now approaching for those in control to relinquish it in favour of more community based decision-making.

There will be a return to people power and consultative decision-making at all levels. The wishes of the people will hold sway, as already they are more frequently.

Many tragedies that have happened have been wakeup calls to bring attention to the inadequacy of present regulations. For example the many mass murders committed with guns obtained by those with no good reason for possessing them bring attention to the horrific law that allows easy access to weapons of destruction.

Due to the many tragedies that have been happening, your world has begun a major shift. There is a changing world order of consciousness. The common man will now question governments' decision-making and their actions on behalf of the people. A new voice will be heard that will change the dynamics of action, and love will ultimately triumph over hate.

It is time to stop the horror and the fear and live in trust, peace and love. The emergence of these issues now is timely, and each needs to be attended to and dealt with. All that has been suppressed for many, many generations now needs to be brought to the surface and eradicated with much wisdom and strength. Just as these issues on the global scale need to be attended to, so too do your own personal suppressions.

Perhaps you have hidden away in your memories feelings of resentment for someone. Now is the time to look at this and handle it. Perhaps by addressing what you were resenting in the actions of this other person you can see the mirror of unworthiness or lack of love within yourself.

As you take out and look at this suppressed memory, all you may need do is write it on paper, give forgiveness to yourself for your painful thoughts and forgiveness to the other person concerned, tear up the paper and burn it with spoken words of letting go accompanying the disappearance of the written words. This will free you to move on for what is to come.

Please understand how powerful meditation is in assisting you to tap into your own Godself and the deepest memories within you. Trust in your worthiness will have increased, with the state of beauty all around you being ever present in your mind's eye. You are now in a position of power and choice.

Much has been written about the Age of Aquarius and the age of change. As this arrives you have noticed, we are sure, the changes in many ways of achieving happiness. Many people are discarding the trappings of materialism and moving towards a simpler, more natural way of being. There is an urgency to create more of this and a very big urgency for you to find your balance *in nature* by communing with it as often as possible.

This is another of the tools that can assist you to move forward with grace and ease. All living things are part of the web of life, and in the roles they play they are contributing to your harmony and wellbeing, just as you can contribute to theirs.

It is essential you give loving attention to the plants in your gardens or, if you live in an apartment block, to your pot plants, which are essential for you if you are to have a connection with nature. As you acknowledge the wonder of their beauty and support them in being as they are meant to be, providing them with ideal conditions for their development and fulfilment of their purpose, you will set up a beautiful web and flow of loving, mutually supporting energy between you.

The same attention applies to the animals and birds as well as rocks and insects in your surroundings. We suggest that as you understand this, the rewards will be there for you all. Create this wonderful environment wherever you are, and especially when you are travelling away from your own established support web of love at home.

In a hotel room it is most important to bring in fresh flowers and enjoy the beauty of nature through them, as this is an artificial world of man-made materials far removed from nature and all things natural.

For those of you who use computers, please bring into your computer room many living plants to balance the strong electromagnetic fields generated by the computer. The plants will need to be rotated to restore their own balance after a week or so. This is most important to maintain your own harmony and balance and retain your now lovely high frequencies. As you tune into your fields of knowledge you will find the world of computers, the internet and television give you far less joy than your own amazing connection to the knowledge of the universal wisdom, which is pure knowledge and guidance for your soul.

You will come to understand that the media and the information channelled through computers generate many falsehoods to maintain control of the masses. We also suggest you will find it far more amusing and satisfying to be in your own powerful position – the one that is unique to you. No one else has access to your own computer link to the divine without your permission, which is not so with manmade computers.

Another most useful tool to bring you to your state of powerful knowing is *the ability to fly.* Yes, we have mentioned this before in other material, and now we want to explore it further with you.

As your body becomes lighter through your frequencies becoming higher, it will lose its density and transform you into a being that is capable of changing and creating an energy substance suitable for any task at hand. If you need to move to another place in a hurry you can create the thought that will change your form to that of a bird; you can then transpose yourself quickly and resume your human form once again on arrival at your planned destination. This is not the teleporting we mentioned earlier. That does not involve your form, only thought.

So we can now tell you that as you become lighter, many new abilities await you. We will talk further of this later in this book.

May thoughts of love be ever-present in all you do. With love the world will become the beautiful place of your dreams and desires, fulfilling your reason for being.

Chapter Three

Have you considered the people in your family who came before you? You possibly never knew your great-grandparents or even your grandparents. They are the forerunners of your present genetic make-up, the carriers of the potential your line of family has always had. Many of you have strong likenesses to your parents, grandparents and so on. You have inherited their genes for physical characteristics and likewise for personality and intelligence.

What is not well known is the inheritance of the spiritual understanding and wisdom of the soul you are. You are another representative of your soul clan here to continue the work they have done to awaken your own soul group to a higher level of God consciousness. Many of your predecessors might have had their truths suppressed, and so lived without fulfilling their mission when they lived that particular life. Never mind, *you* are now here to carry on their incompleted purpose. Perhaps they were very successful in their spiritual achievements, and they have prepared the way for you to go further in understanding the meaning of existence. Whatever your situation, you have within your memory banks all the information and knowledge that are required for you to delve deep and retrieve the wisdom for your awakening to who you truly are.

This knowledge within your cells has been embedded there for the many thousands of years since your genetic line came into being. With much loving curiosity and determination on your part more can be revealed to you in the way of your origins as the human you are now. Not only are you an Australian, American or Englishperson, perhaps with an Irish mother or Scottish father, you are from other parts of the Galaxy with a home there from whence you came.

You are all originally from other star systems that support life continuously, and you earthlings – humans – have come to Earth to experience emotions and love in the way that is particular to this planet.

You needed a physical form to enable you to carry out your purpose, and so here you are in your present form of a body with two legs and arms, a head, eyes, ears and so on. This is the form most suitable for you to gain the experience you need to have.

In other galaxies and homes you did not need the particular physical form you have now, and perhaps you looked very different. Remember, your form is only the vehicle for your soul, and all you need to achieve can occur with utmost respect to it.

With you growing in understanding that you are much more than a three-dimensional physical being, you can utilise the form you have so much more freely and lovingly – in unlimited ways. In reality you are only visiting the Earth as stellar beings of great power and utilising the best means possible to carry out your tasks. Your forebears on the whole did not have the wonderful opportunities you now have, as the Earth was denser and darker in energies.

This is now changing, and humans are here at this time to capitalise on the opportunities for you to transcend the human race and bring it to a higher, more evolved level of being. All your memories are stored within you, not only of your ancestors' wisdom but of the wisdom your own soul has gained from all the other lives you have experienced, both as a human in other times and also during your times in other galaxies.

You have need to tap into your memories of the past to activate the present into becoming the best possible future for you. Can you focus on your abilities to remember the glimpses of forgotten memories that occasionally return in your dreams?

Your dreams are opportunities for your soul to release to you the memories of other times that are quite beyond your present consciousness. Within your dream state you will revisit these times occasionally and, when you focus on this desire as you go to sleep, your dreams will present you with them more vividly and accurately. Keep a journal to record your dreams as you awaken.

With much dedication to focusing on the recollection of your hidden memories, you will soon begin to have much stronger glimpses of the you who is eternal and never-ending in your magnificence of being. As you acquire the skills to bring these memories into your everyday life, the way you live will alter remarkably.

The perceptions you have of the way things are will change, with the knowledge to see beyond the obvious surface intent of the way people go about living their lives and behaving in particular circumstances.

You will have as it were, X-ray vision and thought, picking up on the intentions of every action taken and every idea expressed. With this new ability your way of taking decisions will alter, and everything that happens will be a result of loving creative thought and feeling for the highest good of all. No longer will actions and events be only for those involved to gain personally in the outcome. The outcome will be for the greater good of humanity.

We are with each and every one of you as you surrender your will to merge with the will of the greater consciousness of humanity. With this surrender of the *ego will* comes the *divine will* and with this all can be achieved as is meant to be.

Divine will is very powerful and magical, for in its formation creativity flows into the boundless, limitless areas of thinking, feeling and being to produce outcomes that are far worthier and more beautiful than man can imagine.

In this surrender to the will of God and higher self, you free yourself to live in good grace each day, tapping into the magnificent wisdom of your own memories of the greater self where the answers are all so easily obtained. Your life will flow and create the very best opportunities for you at each turn of the path.

We wish at this time for you to do a little exercise in which you will find these hidden memories of yourself jump into your conscious mind for attention right now. Please relax and sit in a quiet comfortable place with no distraction.

Close your eyes and breathe deeply a few times. As you hear the breath coming in and out, notice the rhythm of it and fully place your attention on it. Allow yourself to sink into the beauty of the rhythm and float to a place of great joy in your mind's eye and in your feeling. As you arrive at this place of beauty and joy notice how you feel and what you see. You may have a feeling of warmth down your spine and see flickering colours or you may feel prickly and see a large hole in your mind.

Whatever the message is, it will be a sign to you of your soul giving you information. This is the beginning of you accessing your soul to gain knowledge and understanding about your greater self, who is there for you always and only needs to be tuned into whenever you desire.

Spend a few moments in this place/space and, as you acknowledge any insights or thoughts that come into your mind or a feeling you receive, gently return to the conscious world and open your eyes when you are ready. Once again, by noting down your message in a journal, gradually a picture will emerge of knowledge you are gaining about yourself. As you trust this process and surrender to divine will in all that happens, the way of access will grow stronger day by day until you have become a strong link in a chain of knowledge being processed by many from the depths of ancient wisdom and now needing to be revealed once again.

Your new beginning will come about gradually, with much change happening without your noticing it. Your cellular structure will become more open and lighter, with the cells having new ways of reacting to the energies surrounding your body. The electromagnetic waves are gaining pace and shortening space-wise so that different receiving modes will be required by all intercepting them.

You need to alter your frequency vibrations to be perfectly in tune with these changes, and this can only happen as you let go of your old ways of thinking about your body and all you do with it, including the way you eat and drink.

Much is written in your newspapers and magazines about the need for such and such types of food and drink to sustain your body and to absorb the essential nutrients so that you have the energy for all you do. However, this is propaganda to create the need for the products available for you to buy.

All you need is love, the energy from the sun and the beauty of your thoughts, along with water of the purest kind and some roughage to aid your digestive system, to process the vital energy you receive from the sun. We say this with the knowledge that your bodies have adapted to the need for the food you now eat, and it will be a while before you readapt to no longer having this need.

The plants and animals you eat of course sourced their energy from the light and warmth of the sun.

The animals have eaten the plants, which have gained their nourishment from their chlorophyll and water, aided and abetted by the minerals and trace elements in the soil.

In the near future you will be able to bypass the plants and animals and go directly to the sun's energy for manufacturing everything you need to live healthily and happily. We have mentioned this in our first book, and now wish to expand on this to show you how to prepare yourself for the time that is soon to arrive.

As your frequencies become lighter, you will begin to have less desire for food, and the cravings will lessen for those favourite snacks that have sustained you in times of stress. As you will be very different in your make-up, your cells will be sustained with light and the air you breathe in.

You will have the ability to transmute the air and light into particles of nourishment. You will extract from the light the chemicals necessary for energy conversion, and likewise from the air you will take in the trace elements vital for sustaining your bodily functions. We know this sounds fanciful and even ridiculous.

However, you need to remember your bodies will no longer be dense and heavy, vibrating at the frequency they are now. Yours will be a very different vehicle form and so you will require different fuel.

This is a return to who you were before you ventured into human form at the beginning of human existence. Human existence has been very necessary in the dense form to create the pathways forward for ancient man's new challenges.

Ancient man created the agenda for you and your previous generations to experience the pitfalls and the joys of creating issues and situations for which collectively the human race has needed to find answers and solutions. Many of the issues have needed great moral integrity to reveal the frailties of the human psyche and bring about resolutions in times of moral crisis faced by entire races of people.

Countless lives have been sacrificed over many centuries to bring about understandings of greed, jealousy, hate, envy and betrayal between people and nations. As yet many have not learned from their forefathers that there is no gain from evil or negative intent, be it on the world or personal scale. Now, however, the human race is going beyond these moral dilemmas, and will move to a new level of experiences from which to learn.

Much will be retained in your cellular memory of the trials and wisdom learnt through this era of humanity's existence, and it will be most useful for you all to utilise in the coming reality. Use your new awareness to spend time in the sun, breathe deeply often and eliminate unnecessary food-eating from your daily habits.

In the near future the way to eat will become very simple and not consume time as it does now. The time saved will be used much more creatively to expand on your feelings of beauty and joy in the experiences of merging into the pure vibrations of colourful energies that are to manifest themselves around you continuously.

This will bring you an expansive feeling of repleteness, and so will eliminate cravings for the comfort you now derive from the eating of food. The pure vibrations in colour energies allow for magical dreaming or hallucination experiences into other dimensions of being.

As you move beyond the physical boundaries of your experiences, you will visit the magical realms of expression of the senses, which will change your perspective of reality.

Colour is the portal into this realm of experience and, as you use your third eye's abilities to capture the essence of each colour you view, much will happen for you to change your own physical structure at the moment of the experience. You will bring into your mind's eye (third eye) all you wish to observe and experience, with many intense colour waves surrounding you and moving through you.

The air will change from 'nothingness' to being full of the beautiful shapes and forms, in vivid colour, of anything you are thinking about. You will only need to think of the most beautiful rose for it to be present in the air.

All these abilities that you will soon have were available to the very first humans on the Earth, and the ability was lost as man neglected his connection with the universal wisdom and love of his God/Goddess within. As man became more physically oriented, he forgot his abilities to enter into other dimensions of himself, and he began to worship false gods external to the divinity within him/herself.

Gradually the abilities inherent in all of you were shut down for most, and only a few retained their ability to connect with their greater, wiser self. However, now the energies are changing again, and you are all being encouraged to remember your forgotten abilities.

We are here with you to assist you to transform yourselves again into the powerful, amazingly adaptable beings you truly are. Can you reinforce this truth with your openness to the various new messages being given to you by many?

Some of these messages may be given to you by strangers who you meet synchronistically for only a short while. However, they may pass on to you a vital revelation about the truth of something occurring or a new piece of the jigsaw about the meaning of your life. Please be alert to these encounters, and understand that the messages being given are from spirit, and the person is acting as a messenger on our behalf.

Chapter Four

In the beginning of time for humanity, many souls volunteered to be part of this experiment to be in human form and live human lives to see how well humanity handled emotions and feelings. This is the crux of your reason for being human.

The early humans were souls from many other levels of existence in other star systems. Much wisdom has been gained over thousands of years of numerous generations of people coming and going into various countries, cultures and races. Souls have returned time and time again to have experiences in a range of circumstances and in different places to add to their vast knowledge and understanding of the diverse array of emotions and feelings there are to experience.

We suggest you yourself may have been here on the Earth as a human countless times, and each time you have added to your infinite wisdom about what it is to be human. We salute your courage in being here at this time of great change, as it is a turning-point in the focus of the experiment. It is a time of drawing on your ancient memories of who you truly are, to go forward into this new phase of existence with all your knowing to draw on.

With your strength, courage and love for all, including yourself, you will have a smooth journey into this time of greater light, love and joy for those who undertake the choice to move through the portal of trust into the existence beyond time and space. With the coming of the present generations of humans, the awareness has returned once again that there is much more to existence than what you can see with your three-dimensional perceptions. In this coming age of even greater awareness will be the opening of the portals into the new awareness of the unlimited opportunities awaiting those who are curious and willing to look beyond all that has been accepted as the norm until now. With your curiosity aroused to delve into the new thinking, beyond the accepted paradigms of daily living, you will gradually accept intuitive thinking, teleporting and telepathy as the normal way to live your life.

Paradigms are there to be moved as soon as the collective consciousness is ready to accept the new as the normal. So you have need to continue to explore and accept what seems to be your own individual truth, putting out your views for the mass consciousness to gradually change. With the wave of new thought and actions happening consistently world wide, the pressure of new ways to live and be will come easily and without evident shock of the new. Collectively mankind now has the circumstances to embrace change in the way you live your life and be fulfilled within it.

It is in being who you truly are that the greatest impact can be made, not in what you are doing to earn a living or how big a house you have. These things are irrelevant in the coming age. It will be how well you think and feel and how beautiful is your aura and kindness.

Your body is your true home this current lifetime, as in the other lives you have lived; however now the importance is no longer in outward manifestations of material possessions but in your 'inward' possessions of all your subtle bodies (emotional, mental and spiritual). Perhaps you have neglected this home of your soul, and now it needs full attention to nurture and feed it with the loving embrace of your thoughts and feelings. Give time to clean it and bring in fresh air continuously, just as you do with the physical house you live in.

We referred earlier to food desires becoming less – and this will be so – and yet you need to continue to feed your soul with loving messages and nurturing stimulation just as the vehicle of your body will need to be fed with physical exercise and fresh air to keep it in order. Emotional nurturing from other sources is very desirable, along with your own loving attention to living in balance and harmony in the beautiful home of your body.

In ancient times man's needs were much simpler, his basic requirements being for shelter, food and warmth. From that time his search has been to continuously find better ways to live and progress in his own stature. Spiritual belief was foremost in his thinking in all he did, and ultimately each community based all its decision-making on what spiritual understanding and rules there were within its culture. So as the human race you have now come to the crossroads in your belief structures.

The religions of the world no longer hold control of the thinking of the majority of people, who have remembered to have their own connection with God. They need to reassess their own paradigms within their churches and let go of much that has become outdated and no longer valid.

With much loving thought, you will now move beyond your present existence into one of surrender to the flow of life, each moment being perfect for you no matter what is happening. As you begin to see the shift away from the rigid belief structures society might have imposed on you, you will feel free to explore these new perceptions of who you truly are and move into creating the path of joy and service that is required of you to fulfill your destiny.

This destiny of yours can only be fulfilled when surrender has occurred of all that is no longer of use to you. Much has been mentioned about the warming of the planet and the changing in the environment due to mankind's disrespect for it. We are in a position to witness these changes from the larger perspective and explain how your planet is a living, breathing energy just as you are.

It is not static, and so it is forever changing and evolving in its form and substance. Throughout millions of years of existence, the Earth has become a stable and reliable home for humankind as well as many other creatures and plants of much magnificence. All have had need to adapt to the habitat they have found themselves in, with gradual mutation happening along the way to adjust to the circumstances and conditions of the time.

Mankind is now having to change and adopt new ways in order to be comfortable in the coming new conditions. The Earth *is* warming and shifting its angle of trajectory, might we say, and so there is coming a time of alteration to the weather patterns, the ocean tides and the climatic factors with regard to plant growth for human consumption.

Much has been blamed on man's disregard for keeping waterways clean and the air pristine, with industries being to blame for all the current pollution. We agree with this statement; however it is man's destiny to evolve and adapt to new surroundings, and in the destruction caused by man is the learning of how precious this planet is to you all. Sometimes extremities of evidence are necessary for the lesson to be remembered well.

Now that the human race is at crisis point in finding solutions to the dilemmas facing you, the new paradigms will be more understood in their implication. Perhaps some serious thought will be brought to bear by many countries as global solutions are found for global problems. Not only are countries finding internal solutions for their individual problems, but they are communicating world wide to find altruistic solutions for the benefit of all. This does not mean you as an individual can sit back and not do your bit. Please attend to your own household circumstances and dispose of your unwanted waste in the most thoughtful way possible, recycling where you can and being considerate with your use of energy and water.

In the near future many more environmentally friendly products will be available, such as new refrigerators and cars, to name but two. We also suggest you visualise your home as a user-friendly place, giving it loving thoughts and gratitude for it being there for you. Talk to your plants and trees and thank them for their beauty and the work they are doing to balance and harmonise your environment. With this loving gratitude, the energy surrounding your home will become beautifully enriched and enable you to have the confidence to trust that all will be well for you no matter what is happening in your town, city or country.

When each of you can do this, the web of love around the world will strengthen, thus assisting to dissipate the pollution and negativity that are holding many people trapped in despair and lack of hope for a better world.

Also ask for assistance from the devas, the angels of the environment who are available to assist when asked in regard to any given problem or dilemma concerning the state of the earth. All you need do is place a special request to them to assist you in whatever you are wishing to see transformed or repaired. It is your trust and loving thoughts directed to them, and gratitude afterwards, that assists them to maintain their magic energies, their transformational abilities.

The Earth is now at the point of choice, just as you are at this point, and, depending on the amount of loving respect and attention offered by mankind, it will choose to destroy itself *or* transform to a place of greater beauty and opportunity for those who also choose to live in love and with love for all they are involved with in their present lives. Can you think deeply about this now please?

The now of your today is the most important moment of your life. As each moment arrives, the way to make the most of it is to bring about awareness of the significance of everything around you and your feelings in this moment and create miracles with your joy of action at this time. As the moment passes, so will another moment arrive, giving you further opportunity to manifest all that is necessary for you to achieve your purpose.

With purpose in every moment, you manifest all that is for your highest good and the greater good of mankind. You have need to be aware of your motives in all you are doing. Are your motives for your own self-advancement or are they to benefit mankind as a whole? When you can honestly act out of concern for the true progress of the collective good you will begin to feel a sense of worthiness in your actions, resulting in a deep sense of peace and serenity within.

This move away from ego-centred actions to altruistic ones brings about a feeling of contentment and release into a space of relief and detachment from the outcome of your actions.

Non-attachment to all you do is another powerful tool to assist you in moving forward in your quest for a new beginning. As you let go of your attachment, not only to your possessions and people in your life but also to the need for your expectations to be fulfilled as you want them to be, you create the beautiful space for everything to happen for your highest good, which will also be for the greater good of mankind in general.

Non-attachment can appear to be a position of coolness or uncaring in regard to what is happening in your life. This is a fallacy, as you can easily be caring and kind; however you can also be *emotionally* detached from whoever or whatever is involved in the issue at hand. In this state of detachment you have the ability to act with wisdom and knowledge of the universal mind, instead of only with your own limited personality mind, which may not have the wisest solution to whatever is being presented.

The universal mind is privy to the true intentions behind any scenario being presented to you, and in relating to it you will find the best answers in regard to how to act or react at the appropriate moment. Emotions are there to learn from and to experience in all forms. However, as you become a being of greater wisdom, you will have fuller understanding of the emotions you experience, and will therefore be able to master them.

This does not mean denying any emotional feelings you have. It means having mastery of them, acknowledging them well and then remaining detached – not allowing them to have control of the way you handle your life.

Overcoming your attachment to your emotions, and allowing the universal mind to support your choice of decisions at *all* times, is a huge step forward in your way towards mastery of who you truly are and why you are on the Earth at this time.

The soul is eternal, as you are eternal, and yet most of you do not acknowledge this. We wish for you to remember this each day before you start your daily work or chores. Remember you are *all* here by choice at this time of new beginnings to assist the evolutionary process to be accomplished smoothly and lovingly. We encourage you all to have the willingness to move forward with trust and confidence, knowing you are supported in your journey. The journey certainly has its trials and disappointments, but these are all there to assist you to develop deeply the understanding of your true nature and worth. As you search within yourself for answers to your deepest yearnings, you may discover many attributes you did not know you had. They come from those hidden memories of you from other lives in previous times. These memories are your deepest truths, to be utilised now for the good of all.

Chapter Five

The new beginning is already happening for you all, and yet so many are not aware of anything different in their feelings about themselves or those around them. These people have not yet turned on their switch to the new, might we say. They have not the awareness to understand there is a whole new existence there for them if they so desire and if they take the time to investigate what is beyond their three-dimensional existence.

They only need to wake themselves up to the parallel existence around them and then choose to take part. As they continue to slumber through their lives, they are missing out on the rewards that are there for them. These rewards are not of the material kind and are known only to those of you who are awake, alert and aware.

Perhaps you have come far on your journey of awakening, and understand fully the rewards we are talking about. These rewards are those of the peace, joy and fulfilment of achieving your purpose as you fully apply yourself to it. With the loving intent, willingness and knowledge of yourself as a being of enormous power and worth, you can detach from the need for rewards from your efforts; however they will be there for you and can be enjoyed fully with modesty and integrity for all to share.

You can assist in nudging those who are still asleep into transforming. Firstly we suggest you have a time of meditation and focus on any particular person who is in need of awakening. In the meditation you can send loving thoughts to this person and encourage them to begin to notice synchronistic happenings in their life. In no way are you to place any directive thoughts there for the person concerned. All you can do is encourage them to be open to noticing things or events. Your encouragement may be the spark to them opening their portal into this parallel world they had no idea existed.

Also by your sharing with them the strange, seemingly coincidental happenings that you experience, they will begin to take note of how well your life seems to be going. They will slowly pay more attention to your ideas and perceptions of events and people, and begin to notice more for themselves. Eventually they may begin to read articles in magazines and books that interest them regarding paranormal happenings and begin to think more deeply about existence. Your role is only to encourage them to be more open and to lead by example.

The new is not really new at all, as it has always existed, though not seen by you before. It is as though you have now graduated to high school after dealing with all your preliminary learning in lower school. High school has always been there, only you were not ready for it until you had graduated from the lower level. High school offers many choices of subject matter and career direction. You are always given a taste of many subjects to learn about before your selection narrows.

This applies also to the new ways of living for the human race. You can sample many ways and ideas, bringing about further understanding of your own field of expertise, before you narrow your choices of endeavour. Your endeavour will be your ultimate purpose for this lifetime. We say those who continue to slumber and fail to fulfil their purpose of truth will find it increasingly difficult to live in harmony with your planet Earth.

As the frequencies speed up, those with the heavier frequencies will find more disharmony in their lives, increasing their susceptibility to disease (dis-ease) and accidental death. Do not mourn the passing of these people, as their choice was not to continue on to the opportunities of the new. They will have opted out of their responsibilities this lifetime, leaving the way open for you and your fellow awakened ones to pave the way forward into the new.

There are those of humankind, however, who have served their purpose, and their cycle of physical life has come to an end naturally. These people will leave of their own accord in the planned way that is their will. We will say they are blessed and happy to leave behind their experiences, with the return to spirit a welcome reward for their time in the material, physical world.

We also must mention the need for you to respect the passing of each one for whatever reason, whether it be the natural conclusion to lives well lived and purposes fulfilled, or whether they are leaving now as they no longer wish to fulfil their intended purpose. Each soul needs to be given the dignity of respectful farewelling, as to have agreed to come into being as a human is indeed a wonderful achievement.

With time you will all have further insight into the workings of the big picture of planning for the human condition to come. As you become lighter and freer, you will indeed become used to your greater awareness and understanding of what you need to create for your own particular destiny to unfold naturally and purposefully.

The new is already in existence all around you in every facet of life. Most of you can tap into this as you change your focus from all that has been familiar and open up your visions, allowing in the unfamiliar world of new senses and visionary objects.There will be strange apparitions and sounds around you that may be tuned into as you change your tuning within your feelings.

All you need do is take a deep breath and let go of the barriers that keep you confined in three-dimensional reality. You will then be receptive to the angelic music and harmonies, and see the vivid colours of energies around you and everyone nearby.

With your willingness to *allow,* you will bring forth these occurrences into your daily life and live continuously amongst the divine musical rhythms, harmonies and melodies, with your visionary delights also being richer in colour and form. When this begins to happen for you, it will be your acceptance of this extra stimulation that will bring you further into the new parallel existence more easily whenever you desire.

You may not always desire it, as you have need to mix with those who are not as advanced as you in opening up. It will be your desire to assist them to move forward that continuously takes you 'back' to the dense reality. Growing more comfortable in this new reality, you will find it no effort to move between the realities when necessary.

Kindness (another tool) is vital to create joy in all you are being and doing. In your kindness to yourself and others you are allowing your divine self to shine forth with authenticity and genuine caring.

Kindness is a forgotten trait with many humans, for they see it as a weakness. They consider that being kind will undermine their authority and control in any situation and show a side of them that they consider secret and vulnerable, and yet kindness is a form of unconditional love that is the ultimate of acts for all mankind. Please consider kindness as a tool of utmost importance in all your being and doing. Bring about random acts of kindness as often as possible, without giving any thought to the consequences. This will assist in bringing to you, and to the person or people concerned, feelings of joy and a greater elevation of your energy fields, which will enable you all to create the perfect conditions for further growth of your souls for the good of mankind as a whole.

Mankind celebrates its existence often in the way of rituals and con-nections with each other in sports and challenges of the business kind. With contact and sharing there are times of rites of passage connected to birth, marriage and death.

At these times man pauses to reflect and measure the state of play, so to speak. Each member of a family, neighbourhood, city or country takes stock of themselves in regard to their fellow family members or citizenship, and does a mental and emotional check of themselves in their contribution or value to society. They unconsciously review their life and resolve to reinforce or improve their position amongst their fellow man.

As you will have noticed, family gatherings especially are full of powerful dynamics, with each family member relating differently with every other member in their own unique way according to their energy dynamics. If there are unresolved conflicts still needing to be dealt with, these family occasions can be opportune times to confront and resolve misunderstandings. All families have many secrets and hidden dynamics, which are there for you to acknowledge and tackle when you are ready. By being ready we mean when you feel wise and understanding enough to reveal your own feelings regarding the issue that is important to you. With the revelation of your own truth on the matter, you can then kindly ask for, or give, forgiveness where necessary, and then let go of long-held resentments. It is in the dealing with and letting go of the issues that is the crux of the matter.

Many families live their entire lives without airing any grievances, and many feelings are left unexpressed. In this way the experiences are not finalised as they are meant to be, and this particular facet of your growth is not fulfilled.

We encourage you all to have a deeper look at your disappointments and misunderstandings within your own nuclear family as well as your extended family of grandparents, parents, cousins and so on, gradually tackling the issues involved in your relationship with each one of them. As you free yourself from those niggly little resentments, perhaps from long ago, you may find a new way to relate to those who have been really difficult to relate to before.

Families are important, and can be very supportive of you and your role here this lifetime, but they can also stifle your progress if they keep you bound within their perhaps limited paradigms for living life. It is up to you to break free from their influence, unless it is influence that is in harmony with your own ideals and wisdom.

Often your choice of family has been one to overcome and challenge its views and values so you can be very clear in your own destiny choice. Often you are challenged in your own personality (ego state) to choose between the status quo within or to branch away and be true to your soul's knowing of the truest path for you.

Within your family are many members of your soul clan who are with you to provide you and themselves with the very best opportunities for growth in understanding of all your souls. Whether they are loving and kind or difficult and harsh, they are all playing their perfect roles to assist you to overcome the very problematical dilemmas they represent or create for you. As you understand this you can let go of any anger, hurt or resentment towards each person, and acknowledge the challenge to overcome whatever needs resolving without being emotionally drained or damaged. Be detached in your approach to resolution, and with unconditional love you will let go and move on very easily.

Chapter Six

Perhaps you consider your way forward to be full of difficulties and hurdles. You may be right in this, but as you transmute your feelings towards multidimensional acceptance of who you truly are – and know you are only playing a role, once again, as a human in this lifetime of yours as you have done many times before – you will have more understanding of your difficulties and why you need to experience them.

You will indeed have a very different perception of the intent behind what is happening, and find your resolutions with grace and ease in the choices you make regarding the handling of the problem or dilemma. You will find you do not waste energy dwelling on the issue, and trust will be there in every thought you have about it.

With trust and divine acceptance in acknowledging the so-called problem, you will free yourself from attachment to the outcome that may or may not occur. You will allow divine intervention to assist in bringing about the very best outcome for your highest good. This will also be the outcome that is best for all others concerned in the situation.

Trust and non-attachment always go hand-in-hand in your everyday living, and your ability to accept that the flow of energy around you can be pure and positive will make it so.

You are the co-creator of your existence, along with God/Goddess, and in your partnership you have a very powerful team. Much of the time you let down this partnership with your lack of trust that there can be a positive outcome in every situation.

Do you consider God/Goddess needs to do your work for you? You are a partnership, and you need to have mutual respect, love and cooperation continuously between you.

An open dialogue is very necessary, and in your times of silence and meditation the answers and solutions become very clear and mutual acceptance for the actions needing to be taken can be achieved.

We remind you you are God/Goddess within, and so all it takes is for you to consult within yourself to find the best resolutions for all you undertake.

We can now go back to the family dynamics we have just spoken of and suggest you apply this trust and non-attachment when dealing with your family interactions. As you remember you are individual members of a group of souls here in the physical form to experience emotions and feelings, you can detach from any obligation to fulfil other family members' requirements of you if they are not for your highest good or part of your soul's desire.

In breaking free from feelings of dutiful obligation within the family hierarchy, you will be free to choose to be in relationship with any one or more members in your own self-expressive way, without the former expectations and perceived obligations. Your free will offers you the opportunity then to experience this relationship in the way that is divinely planned.

As you create only loving, joyful and enriching relationships in your life, you can let go of many who do not serve your purpose or vision. They will also benefit from your detachment from them, as they will see the need to create their own more fulfilling relationships for themselves.

When this happens, each of you will discover that each day is rewarding and nurturing in all ways.The path will be clearly marked with signs of confirmation of your ability to live with greater authenticity and truth.

With great respect we wish now to remind you again of the roles you will be playing in the future. You will indeed not have to perform as dramatically as you may have in the past to create the emotional responses between you all.

The future will bring you to a position of refinement and grace, with your emotional interplay being a respectful and intelligent exchange of understanding. The time will be there for you to pursue more intellectual investigation into the nature of existence, and the quest for knowledge of the greater understanding will be very evident.

Opportunities will be there for you all to experience multidimensional information and explore many other ways of being. In experiencing telepathy, teleporting and holographic exploration of your senses, you will indeed let go of your limited perception of what your existence is. Expansion of yourself to live fully and continuously in your multidimensional and multifaceted awareness will release you all from your previous understanding of what it is to be human.

There will be a new definition of what being a human is. To be human in the coming new existence is to be a sensory being of light in a form of physical matter that can transform at will from physicality to etheric density when required to serve the purpose at hand. Your form will be flexible in its shape as well as weight to meet the needs of each moment. And the senses you possess will expand to include intuitive, clairvoyant, clairaudient and clairsentient abilities as normal instead of their being thought of as unusual.

Everyone will have expanded use of their senses along with heightened perceptual abilities and instant understanding in every moment. You will recognise each other by your energy colours and the patterns in which your colours have presented themselves. Each person will possess a unique arrangement of the colours, much as you all have unique fingerprints.

Visually you will all present a beautiful arrangement of colour patterns weaving in and out as you intermingle. Much will be understood between you by your thoughts being displayed in your colour patterns, and verbal language will not be as necessary.

The way you move will be through floating, since you will not be as heavy; and with a thought you will project yourself to where you wish to be.

This will occur gradually over much time, until future humans accept the use of these abilities as very normal behaviour. With willingness, trust and awareness, however, you can manifest much of this for yourself when you focus your intent on it. We suggest manifestation of all you wish to create and co-create can happen when you believe in it enough.

Your subtle bodies are waiting in readiness for instructions from you in your physical body to allow them full share in your existence. Each subtle body is an individual part of you, and yet they are all intertwined to work as a team assisting in your alignment with your God/Goddess within, as well as to create harmony and balance in alignment with the universal wisdom and knowing.

The more you acknowledge you are grander and more expansive than your physical body, the more easily you will enter into your multidimensional beingness whenever required. This ability will become a natural state as each and every one of you moves into the greater awareness of yourselves as beings of powerful potential and great knowing.

As the wave of new understanding arrives in your thinking, collectively, many of you will notice a new approach to your analysis of much that has been ignored by you up till now. The way of perceiving your life will be changed forever as you surrender to the new knowledge now accessible to you.

This will actually be knowledge you have held within your cells for eons of time, and you can now tap into it again as the 'time' is here for you to utilise it once more, with the conditions perfect for application of all that is sacred and beautiful.

Acknowledgment of new thought forms – or, might we say, ancient knowledge now resurfacing – will assist you all to move into a higher dimension and new state of being with great ease. Within this knowledge will be memories of your many experiences throughout the many lives you have lived, and yet you will have no need to retain the pain, resentment or whatever else you might have endured in these lives.

All you need do is remember the wisdom gained through having these experiences; indeed you will be full of great understanding of the struggles mankind has endured in order to evolve. And in your own individual soul are encoded your personal struggles and sacrifices, as well as the grand achievements and feelings of love and joy experienced by you.

The time is now here for you to apply this wisdom in your new existence. Streamline your *doing* and concentrate on your *being*.

In being who you truly are at this time you will manifest the highest form of assistance to others who are following your lead. As we have said before, you are to become beacons of light to show others the way, and this can only be by example and encouragement. Others will only follow when they are ready and know of their need to grow.

The opportunity is here for us to encourage you to move beyond your paradigm of living complex lives and to regard yourselves as energy more than dense form in a human shape, as now your shape will be far more malleable and changeable to suit the need of your requirements in each moment.

If it suits you to be visible in human form, so you will be. If it suits you to become invisible physically, so you will be. Nothing will be set in concrete so to speak.

You are a limitless, timeless and spaceless entity who will once again have the ability to move in many ways, depending on your needs. Please understand it is your own thinking and beliefs that will free you from your previous limited way of thinking and believing.

Remember you are unique, and master of your own glorious and powerful destiny, which will contribute greatly to the ongoing success of the ever-changing state of mankind.

Chapter Seven

Creating the best future for yourself begins with your truth being revealed to you. We have discussed this previously, and by now you will know your truth is who and what you truly are as an essence. That part of you is pure and beautiful always, and does not succumb to the whims of fashion, current attitudes or thought. It is the deepest part of you, the part that *knows*. You know what you know and there is no need to analyse why or how.

It is your knowing – the wisdom from your collective lives and genes. You have stored all the knowing from all your previous experiences in many lives as well as all the wisdom from your direct lineage for many generations.

This is the truth we wish you to acknowledge and utilise. Please disregard unsuitable behaviour patterns in this lifetime and go into your deepest wisdom, *remembering all that your heart knows,* which has not always been heard. As you sit in the silence you will hear it speak with messages so clear and wise that you will wonder why you have not always listened carefully before. We remind you this is the first step to recovering your memories of all your knowing for eternity. As you continue to delve into your self-knowing, more and more will be revealed of all that is you. You may be drawn to read certain books and articles and/or watch documentaries on television about archaeology – the many discoveries of ancient cities and peoples. These will be wake-up calls to explore further. Sometimes you will resonate well with what you read or see, and it may be a trigger to remember you were there in that experience in a past life. You may be curious to know more, and so go on a journey of discovery about that particular life.

With your collective knowledge growing, the opportunity will be there to truly awaken to all the wisdom you possess. This will activate body cells to transform so that you can begin to utilise all your knowing in this present life. The opportunity will then come for activation of this wisdom in your day-to-day life, with great changes coming into play for all you are being and doing. The perceptions you have of reality will change, with you viewing this life as an opportunity to further your wisdom in whatever way is appropriate.

Senses will be heightened and expanded to envelop the new vibrations of love and compassion within – and without also. The world of your making will become less stressful and more enjoyable. The challenges will be of the mind and not of the body or emotions. The mind will have expanded to the point that it receives more intelligence and beauty of thought than you have ever conceived possible. Fear will dissolve, and you will begin to live with complete joy and trust that your journey is one of creative expansion of all you are thinking and feeling for the betterment of all humankind, and not only yourself as an individual soul.

The sense of oneness with every living thing and every being will be heightened, and the sense of rapport with all that is will bring beautiful harmony and balance to your own corner of the world. Opening up to your true wisdom will indeed create a world of beauty and harmony. Peace will at last be a reality for humankind. As the fear within dissolves, so will the fear without dissipate. Fear creation will no longer hold sway and, as it loses its power over many, so the planet may at last come to be a place of true loving vibrations, with kindness, consideration for all and harmony prevailing. All it will take is for each individual to find the truth of their soul and then live accordingly to bring about peace and enjoyment for humankind.

Are you now fully aware of your own potential? And do you know you have limitless possibilities for creating the powerful future you wish for your own soul's advancement? All you need do is *allow*. Allow yourself to float free and *detach* from past expectations of who you think and feel you are and surrender to the universal plan you have within your essence.

This plan is in seed form, only needing to be fertilised and watered to grow into the great creation of your highest intentions. We say you have placed this seed within eons ago, and have been waiting for the conditions to be ideal for the fruition to come. The time is here to manifest your calling and deepest knowing. Do not hesitate – be bold, courageous and unswerving in opening up the floodgates to allow out all you are in your most glorious beingness.

The old ways are no longer relevant in the coming climate of changing paradigms for living. With trust and detachment from previous expectations of your self-realisations you can be led forward into the ideal situation for experiencing growth in your understanding of the connection between every living thing and every being.

We are all energy expressing a different aspect of God in our own individual way. Each way is equal to every other way and yet unique, commanding respect and honour no matter what the expression is. We ask you to honour and accept yourself and every other facet of expression without criticism or judgment. Everything *just is*. Everything *is as is,* and accepting this is how you will reach your level of self-mastery.

In coming to this level of understanding, you have taken a giant leap forward towards assisting the many who are continuing to discover this. As you have this awareness, and this allowance for all to be as it is, living with the flow of energy surrounding you and the acknowledgement of your own unique and valuable role, much will become apparent regarding the need to fulfil your purpose. Your seed within will grow magnificently as it matures with attention and love.

Now are coming the perfect conditions for you to act on your true plan and purpose. All old desires and wants will no longer have any importance, and revealed in their place will be your deepest passions, which you will truly fulfil. All you have come into physical form to accomplish will indeed come about with effortless ease. Memories of who you truly are as an essence – an aspect of God – will be revealed, and can be the cause for much celebration as you move into knowingness of what it is you have a calling to do.

Have you considered that your true expression may be simply to be happy and sing? Many of you feel and think your life is a failure when you have not become the successful doctor or lawyer others might have expected you to become. Perhaps your realisation and purpose are to reject those expectations and be true to yourself in whatever way. This may be your biggest challenge this lifetime – you being true to *you* no matter what the expectations have been.

Allowing yourself to forgive others and yourself for all that has occurred that is not for anybody's highest good – or the good of your nation – will free your spirit to soar high into the realms of beauty and love. This love that is within has need to be freed and expressed unconditionally, with no thoughts of resentment or hurt remaining.

Forgiveness for all things, actions and people will bring you the wisdom that has been locked away within your cells and that can be acted upon now to transmute your energies into those of the belovedness of creation. This will bring you to the state of mastership and the highest level of knowing. Please let go and surrender to the creative process of eternal love, forever bringing you to a higher place within your heart. The unconditional love of your heart will open the doors to the dimensional portal where you can enter into new phases of growth for your soul and bring forward the awareness that you have denied yourself for so long. This awareness will bring with it the new perception of your role; no longer will you be stuck at your previous level of existence. Can you see how easy the transformation will be as you allow yourself to forgive everything that has hurt you and understand that *you* chose those experiences for your soul to learn more about who you truly are?

We say *letting go* is a key towards your new state of beingness. It will be a major stepping-stone upward and forward. Within yourself lies the key to the wonderful memories of the greater self, and much use will now be made of these memories to set the conditions for placing all your knowing into service, assisting those others only beginning their journey within.

This will take courage, determination and willingness to reveal who you truly are, with readiness to stand firm as doubts may be suggested about what you now stand for. However always remember you are an eternal being, and all that is occurring in the physical dimension is illusory.

Your confidence and strong truth of knowing will dispel any negativity that may come your way. Those who project negative energy towards you are merely unsure of their own truth and therefore wish to protect themselves. Their protection needs to become loving and nurturing. This will then transform them also into beings of higher truth.

Patience is one more most important tool for unlocking your hidden memories. You cannot reveal all of your knowing at one time or within one experience. We therefore wish you to be gentle on yourself and allow slowly, slowly, the unfolding of this understanding of all you are. There is need for consolidation and receptivity within, so you *become* and live this new knowing. Only then are you ready for further understanding to be revealed and assimilated into your outer consciousness.

Your patience may be tested, with many periods of seeming inactivity in your spiritual development. However, much is occurring around and within you in preparation for the next phase of growth as you consolidate your present level of awareness. This test of patience is most crucial in preparation for coming responsibilities. It is only with the wisdom of experience that you will be equipped to assist the many others whose patience will also be tested. It is in the waiting that new insights and perceptions are revealed so that your understanding becomes so much deeper and more relevant.

Have you the willingness and openness to allow your memories to assist this new beginning? The *willingness* to become who you truly are is another powerful tool towards advancement into this parallel world of loveand-light-filled energy, with the ability to let go of previous thoughts about how to live life and the beginnings of surrender into greater connection with your divine/higher self. The way will be open to create much of your vision and manifest the purpose of this visit to the physical plane of being.

Are you willing to leave behind many people in your life who no longer have a strong connection and uphold all you represent? Are you willing to be available to be directed by your soul towards perhaps a new country, city or country town where your services may be required? Many of you are being called to an area of the planet where you are most needed and have agreed on your soul level to go.

It is your *willingness to detach* from all that has supported and comforted you previously and to move forward into the unknown that will bring the fulfilment of your destiny. In the letting go and the *willingness to let go* of all material things, beliefs, attitudes and judgments you will find liberation, at the same time creating the void into which will come the new and valuable conceptual understandings and instructions about what you have chosen to achieve in the future. It is this opening up to grander visions of your own role that will create the opportunities that now await you. Spirit cannot assist unless you are willing to allow this help, and this requires cooperation and teamwork between us all. Many a time you will be asked to take the risk of moving into the unknown depths of your mind or feelings, with you venturing into areas you may initially experience as foreign. However, in taking the risk to venture there, you may discover delights awaiting you that have been experienced before in another lifetime, forgotten by your present self.

We are continuously urging you to be creative in thinking and feeling in order to awaken your sleeping potential within. Know this, and each time you have a new idea explore it and take action. We will have planted the seed of this idea for you to act on.

Beyond your physical self at your moment of reading this are all your other selves, who are the different facets of your potential. As we have explained earlier, it is in the recognition of each facet of yourself being equally valid that you can live harmoniously in all dimensions.

In letting go the perception that you are a personalitydriven human being, you will find the ability to alter your persona, depending on the situation at hand, to enable you to weave the magic required to assist those you are to help. By this we mean you will always have the perfect energy vibration for what is necessary. The blending of your own powerful and beautiful energy with whoever you are assisting will indeed heal and bless the recipient.

You will not need any special skills. Being you in your multidimensional awareness will suffice, creating the perfect conditions for all that needs to be done. Loving thoughts, willingness and allowance are the most powerful things you can offer to bring about healing on your planet.

We wish for you to truly learn the ability to *detach* emotionally from all that is occurring around you. We have previously discussed this. In detachment from three-dimensional dramas and issues, you live in the dimension of love and understanding – understanding that the drama or issue is a creation of the person or people involved to bring about their growth on the soul level.

As you live more fully with soul wisdom, these occurrences will disappear from the realm of what you consider important, and so whatever happens will be of no consequence to you. Remember: all is as in a play, with everyone acting out their roles to find their own truths of being.

Detachment from any expectation of outcomes being a certain way will free you to allow the best possible outcome to arrive for you. This will assist you to continue the journey towards your new beginning with ease and much delight.

All it will take is detachment from *how* you expect your creative thinking to lead you to your desired outcome. The Universe/God has the grand overview of how best to bring about fulfilment for your individual purpose in the play of life.

Can you detach also from your *need* to belong? By this we mean the need to belong to organisations, clubs and groups of friends. This does not mean you must live in isolation. If you are a member of a group or organisation detach from the collective thinking and group decisions. Remain an independent thinker within the group and *lead,* do not follow. Remain true to your own knowing and become an inspiration to others, with clear and individual views. Many belong to groups to feel safe and secure, surrendering their own truths purely to be accepted.

By being courageous and confident in your own wisdom, speaking your truth with no attachment to any particular outcome, you will be listened to with respect and interest.

Can you also detach from the need to become successful in whatever you are passionate about? It is not approval from others that will help you feel successful; it is the approval you give yourself as you achieve your dreams and visions. It is detaching from the importance to you of what other people or groups of people may think that frees you to continue to follow your passion for *you*.

This is your soul's way of encouraging you on towards the fulfilment of your purpose here, and assisting you to continue to unravel the hidden memories of the talents and skills within. Not for others but for yourself. Non-attachment is another expression we have used to help you to understand your greater self. Non-attachment means remaining free of feelings of obligation and duty beyond those you feel deeply are necessary. In your freedom to change all you have been and done, this non-attachment to previous obligations and patterns of behaviour will bring about transformation very rapidly.

Non-attachment to all you possess will allow you to move very quickly as need be when the circumstances require it. Being able to let go of people, ideas and possessions when necessary, having no emotional attachment to them, will enable you to go to, and act on, all that is awaiting you in your new beginning, as you are ripe for this to occur.

The lightness of your energy will enable you to flow free of the denseness of your physical being, and re-create yourself as a being of superb beauty and great power. The love you exude will encompass all in your surrounds and, as you have no attachment to all that was previously considered important, you will discover you can have everything, as you wish, by magical manifestation.

Our message of being detached from so much does not mean you are to detach from love of yourself or others. Quite the contrary. It is the detachment from being involved emotionally with your issues, and those of others, that allows you to have unconditional love and non-judgement of everything that happens.

As you become detached from the chaos or drama around you, your power of insight and observation will become heightened and most accurate as to the truth of the matter. This will enable you to be of more assistance, and more balanced in your understanding of your own actions and reactions and those of others you are observing. This brings you to a level of mastery and wisdom where you transcend the lower physical vibrations and create harmony and peace around you, allowing manifestation of healing energies to bring about any necessary changes, full of love.

Detachment does not create separation of one human from another. Detachment is a state of beingness where your *emotional* energy field does not merge with the energy field of emotion of another, keeping your beauty and serenity intact and not allowing distorted vibrations to upset your own.

We are all connected, and each of us a different expression of the God / Universal Energy creating the experiences for us all to grow and expand in knowingness. This does not mean, however, that you need to experience what others are here to learn from, when it is not part of *your* script. Discernment and detachment will keep you focused on your own wonderful journey of discovery.

We are now creating a blessing around you, dear reader, as your journey with us through this book is nearly over. And as we say farewell we wish you to honour who you are in all ways. Remember you are truly unique in your own essence, and the journey you have undertaken to be here reading this text may have been hard and uncomfortable. At times you might have wondered about the reason for all your struggles. We say to you now: know that the reason is to assist mankind collectively to understand him/herself as an expression of God and to discover more about creation. We congratulate you on your courage to undertake this journey of discovery at this most transformational moment in the history of mankind. These efforts to find out more about the meaning of your life are contributing greatly to the lifting of the frequency vibrations of all. These efforts have not been and will not be in vain.

With continuing trust, patience and willingness to walk the path towards the light of your truth, the circumstances will come for your upliftment – the state of Heaven on Earth.

The transition will be complete, and all who have chosen *love* over fear, and who have been willing to risk their unknown future, trusting they will always be supported and encouraged by God and many loving spiritual beings, at last will find themselves in the place of all-knowing and beauty beyond what is imaginable. This will be the age of Golden Light and Love, and all who arrive will indeed know they are at last home.

Namaste

I honour the place in you
in which the entire universe dwells.

I honour the place in you which is of love,
of truth, of light, and of peace.

When you are in that place in you,
and I am in that place in me,
we are one.

Vaisseau

63

Merriene Scott welcomes
your correspondence.
Please contact her at

Email: merriene@merrienescott.com
www.merrienescott.com

www.ingramcontent.com/pod-product-compliance
Lightning Source LLC
Chambersburg PA
CBHW061431050726
47593CB00006B/2316